Condoleezza Rice

Condoleezza Rice

NATIONAL SECURITY ADVISOR

CHRISTIN DITCHFIELD

FRANKLIN WATTS
A Division of Scholastic Inc.
New York Toronto London Auckland Sydney
Mexico City New Delhi Hong Kong
Danbury, Connecticut

Photographs © 2003: AP/Wide World Photos: cover, 14, 17, 38, 50, 71, 73, 76, 86, 97; Corbis Images: 40 (Morton Beebe), 68 (Kraft Brooks), 78 (Kevin Lamarque/Reuters), 30 (Matthew McVay), 81, 90, 102 (Reuters NewMedia Inc.), 48 (Shepard Sherbell), 2 (Emilie Sommer/AFP Photo), 19, 57, 92; Corbis Sygma: 70 (Steve Liss), 62 (Frederick Neema); Getty Images: back cover ghost, 83 (David Bohrer/The White House), 100 (Reuters), 88; Courtesy of Marilyn Banwell Stanley and the Rice family photo collection: 6, 8 top, 8 bottom, 10, 12, 23, 25, 44, 46, 55, 74; Stanford News Service/Linda A. Cicero: 59; Stockphoto.com/Fred Ward: 11; University of Denver, Special Collections: 28.

Library of Congress Cataloging-in-Publication Data

Ditchfield, Christin.
  Condoleezza Rice : National Security Advisor / by Christin Ditchfield.
    p. cm. — (Great life stories)
Summary: A biography of Condoleezza Rice, professor, author, and National Security Advisor to President Bush. Includes bibliographical references and index.

ISBN 0-531-12307-3

1. Rice, Condoleezza, 1954—Juvenile literature. 2. National Security Council (U.S.)—Biography—Juvenile literature. [1. Rice, Condoleezza, 1954– 2. National Security Council (U.S.)—Biography. 3. Women—Biography.] I. Title. II. Series.

UA23.15.D578 2003
355'.033073'092—dc21

2003004640

Contents

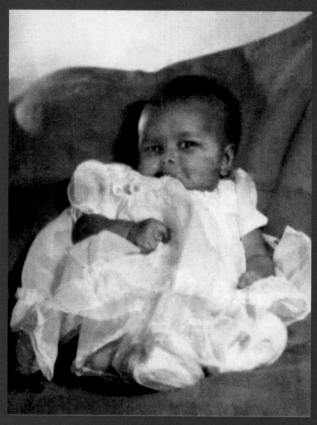

Little did Condi's parents know that that their little girl would grow up to become a very powerful figure in U.S. politics.

A Special Little Girl

On November 14, 1954, John and Angelena Rice welcomed their first and only child into the world. Actually, Angelena was the only one at the hospital—John was delivering his Sunday sermon at the morning church service. He was a minister who also worked as a high school guidance counselor and football coach. John had hoped to have a son—a boy who would be named after him and who would grow up to be an All-American linebacker for the University of Notre Dame. Angelena was a high school teacher who loved opera and classical music. When the baby turned out to be a girl, Angelena created a special name for her. She took the Italian musical phrase *con dolcezza*, which means "to perform with sweetness," and changed the spelling to "Condoleezza."

Condi's parents, John and Angelena, always supported her pursuit of her interests, including playing the piano.

"LITTLE STAR"

From the beginning, John and Angelena believed their daughter, nicknamed Condi, was a very special little girl. "Condi doesn't belong to us," John told a friend. "She belongs to God." The Rices were convinced that somehow, some way, their daughter would accomplish great things and make a difference in the world. Condi's parents wanted her to have every opportunity. If she showed interest in any activity, they encouraged her to give it a try. Condi started taking piano lessons when she was only three years old. With her grandmother as her teacher, she learned to read music before she could read words.

"The first song I learned to play was 'What a Friend We Have in Jesus,'" Condi remembers. "And then I learned to play 'Amazing Grace.'"

People were amazed by the tiny girl's talent. Perhaps she was destined to become a classical musician—a concert pianist. John nicknamed his daughter "Little Star." In addition to the piano, Condi learned to play the flute and the violin. She took tap dance and ballet lessons. When Condi was six years old, her mother bought her a recording of the famous opera *Aida*. Angelena wanted Condi to experience many different kinds of art and culture. The Rices were not wealthy, but they worked hard. They saved every penny they earned to make it possible for their gifted daughter to pursue her dreams.

Although John and Angelena had great expectations for her, Condi never felt pressured by her parents. "They saw no limits for me. They wanted to give me everything. But the most important thing they gave me was unconditional love," she says. "Every night I pray and say, 'Thank you, God, for giving me the parents You gave me.' I was so fortunate to have these extraordinary people as my parents."

On Sundays, John preached at the Westminster Presbyterian Church. Angelena played the organ, and Condi sang along with the choir. It was quite a sight. "My mother was a stunningly beautiful woman," Condi says. "She liked to dress well. She believed in being proper." Angelena wasn't the only one. Friends of the family remember that Condi always looked like a princess—always neat and spotless and never a hair out of place.

It was after church that things got rough. John decided to teach his little girl all about football. Every Sunday afternoon, Condi and her father watched football games on television. They talked about statistics and strategies. They debated different game plans. Then the two of them headed to the backyard to play the "Rice Bowl," their very own football championship. Condi absolutely loved it. "My mother learned to like football in self-defense," she remembers.

During the week, Condi kept busy practicing her music, taking dance lessons, and studying French. She also managed to find time to play with the other little girls in her neighborhood. One of them had a chalkboard in her garage. Sitting in front of the board with their dolls and stuffed animals, the girls played "school." Often, Condi was the teacher.

THE KEY TO SUCCESS

Growing up, Condoleezza heard a lot about the importance of doing well in school. She says, "My parents had a deep and abiding faith in

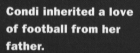

Condi inherited a love of football from her father.

God, they had a deep and abiding faith in family, and they fundamentally believed that education was what counted." And it wasn't just because they were both teachers. John and Angelena Rice believed that education was the key to overcoming the limitations placed on African Americans in the late 1950s and early 1960s.

Although slavery had been abolished almost one hundred years earlier, African Americans were still treated like second-class citizens in most places. It was thought that they were somehow less intelligent than people of other races. Things were particularly bad in the South, where slavery had been a major part of the social and economic system. The Rices lived in the segregated community of Birmingham, Alabama. In Birmingham, blacks and whites lived separately from one another. There were schools for black children and schools for white children, and water

Discrimination against African Americans in the South took many forms, including being forced to use separate facilities from those used by white people, such as water fountains and waiting rooms.

fountains for black people and water fountains for white people. Blacks had to sit in the back of city buses. They could not use restrooms in public buildings. They were not allowed to enter many stores, restaurants, and hotels. Other businesses required blacks to use separate entrances or remain in separate parts of the buildings, away from white customers.

The laws of the land supported this discrimination. They said it was okay for towns to have separate facilities for blacks and whites, as long as they were "equal." But the facilities usually were not equal. Blacks got the worst of everything.

As Condi grew up, her parents tried to shield her from the abuse many African Americans suffered. They raised her in a warm, loving, close-knit community. Their neighborhood was full of people who were determined to achieve their potential, regardless of the challenges they faced. Like their neighbors, the Rices refused to think of themselves as victims. Condi says, "My parents convinced me that though I might not be able to get a hamburger at Woolworth, I could be president of the United States if I wanted to be."

Condi attended a black church and a black school. She lived in a

As a young girl, Condi learned from her parents how to stand up against prejudice. This is a photograph of Condi when she attended Lane Elementary School.

SCHOOL DAYS 1961-62
LANE ELEM.

middle-class black neighborhood. She didn't have much contact with the white community at all. Still, there were times when she felt the sting of racism. Once, Angelena took Condi shopping for a new dress at a department store. An employee would not let Condi try on the dress in the "whites only" dressing room. She told the little girl to go and change in a back storage closet. Angelena was not one to take orders from a salesperson. She informed the woman, "My daughter will try on this dress in a dressing room, or I'm not spending my money here." When it became clear that Angelena would not back down, the embarrassed employee motioned them to a proper dressing room.

On another shopping trip, seven-year-old Condi brushed up against an expensive hat. The white saleswoman snapped, "Get your hands off that hat!" Angelena boldy replied, "Don't you talk to my daughter that way!" She turned to her little girl and said sweetly, "Now Condoleezza, you go and touch every hat in this store." Condi cheerfully obeyed. Time

Dr. Martin Luther King, Jr.

Dr. Martin Luther King, Jr. was one of the most influential leaders of the Civil Rights Movement. He inspired blacks and whites to work together for racial equality. He directed nonviolent protests in the South. In 1964, King was awarded the Nobel Peace Prize. In one of his most famous speeches, he said: "I have a dream that my four little children will one day live in a nation where they will not be judged by the color of their skin, but by the content of their character." Sadly, Dr. King was assassinated on April 4, 1968. The whole nation mourned his death.

and time again, Condi saw her parents stand up to racism and refuse to be intimidated by others' prejudice. It gave her the confidence to stand up for herself.

PREACHING THE VALUE OF EDUCATION

The Civil Rights Movement began in the 1950s. All over the country, people who opposed segregation began protesting in the streets. African Americans organized boycotts, refusing to ride on segregated buses. They stopped shopping in stores where they were treated disrespectfully. People marched through towns, carrying signs and banners that condemned racism. They demanded that unfair laws be changed.

John and Angelena Rice believed in freedom and equality for all people. But for the most part, they did not participate in protests. "My

A group of protestors picket outside Birmingham businesses. Protests and sit-ins in Birmingham helped bring attention to the Civil Rights Movement.

father was not a march-in-the-street preacher," Condi recalls. The Rices' community had a different strategy. "They all thought America would get better," Condi says. "They had faith that by the time we were older, things were going to open up. That whole generation of parents in Birmingham was determined that they would educate and expose their kids to the finer things in life, so that when America opened up, their kids would be ready."

Black parents and teachers taught their children that, because of prejudice, they had to be "twice as good as white kids to stay even—and three times as good to get ahead." They had to work hard at everything. They could not make excuses for being lazy or undisciplined. As a guidance counselor, John Rice regularly visited the homes of his students. He talked to parents about how they could prepare their children for college. He explained what subjects they needed to study and what tests they had to take. He took busloads of students on field trips to college campuses. Some of his neighbors called the preacher an "education evangelist." In his spare time, John supervised after-school sports and other activities he thought would help his students develop into mature, well-rounded adults.

In the summers, John accepted teaching positions at colleges around the country. Angelena and Condi traveled with him. "Other kids went on vacation to Yellowstone National Park. They took car trips to see national monuments. We stopped on college campuses," Condi recalls. "We once drove 100 miles out of our way to Columbus, so that I could see Ohio State University."

Higher education was particularly important to Condoleezza's parents, both of whom had college degrees. They taught Condi about their family history and explained how education had helped her grand-parents escape the poverty and despair that other African Americans experienced. Condi later shared that story with others:

> Grandaddy Rice was the son of a farmer in rural Alabama, but he recognized the importance of education. Around 1918, he decided he was going to get book-learning. And so, he asked, in the language of the day, where a colored man could go to college. He was told about little Stillman College, a school about 50 miles away. So Grandaddy saved up his cotton for his tuition and he went off to Tuscaloosa.
>
> After the first year, he ran out of cotton and he needed a way to pay for college. Praise be, as He often does, God gave him an answer. My grandfather asked how those other boys were staying in school, and he was told that they had what was called a scholarship. And they said that if he wanted to be a Presbyterian minister, then he could have one, too. Grandaddy Rice said, 'That's just what I had in mind.' And my family has been Presbyterian and college-educated ever since!

TRAGEDY IN BIRMINGHAM

As the Civil Rights Movement grew, so did tension between blacks and whites. Often, peaceful protests became violent as protesters clashed with police. Once or twice, Condoleezza's parents took her to see a march or hear a speech. The country was changing. History was being made. The Rices wanted their daughter to be aware of what was happening. However, most of the time, they kept her far away from what they considered to be dangerous situations. It wasn't easy. Some of the most controversial events of the Civil Rights Movement took place in Birmingham. Some whites tried to frighten black demonstrators and keep them from speaking up. They attacked and killed African Americans who were traveling alone. They set fire to black homes and churches.

On September 15, 1963, Condi's father was delivering his Sunday sermon. Suddenly, the congregation heard the sound of a distant explosion. Two miles (5.2 kilometers) away, a group of white men had bombed the Sixteenth Street Baptist Church. Four young girls, ranging in age from eleven to fourteen years old, were killed. Condi was nine years old then. She knew two of the girls, Cynthia Wesley and Denise McNair. Cynthia had lived next door to the Rices. Denise had been in Condi's kindergarten class.

The bombing of the Sixteenth Street Baptist Church killed four young girls (left to right): Denise McNair, Carole Robertson, Addie Mae Collins, and Cynthia Wesley. Condi knew Denise and Cynthia.

Condi recalls being very sad about the death of her friends. She attended the memorial service and watched the small caskets being taken to the cemetery for burial. Somehow, the bombing didn't frighten Condi. She was not worried that something like that would happen to her. "My parents were pretty good at giving the impression that they could protect me from that, even if they couldn't," she says. "I remember being more scared by the Cuban Missile Crisis, because that was something I was sure my parents couldn't protect me from."

In 1964, President Lyndon B. Johnson signed the Civil Rights Act. Segregation was no longer legal. The United States government declared that all citizens had the same rights and privileges under the law, regardless of the color of their skin. The Rices watched the announcement on

The Cuban Missile Crisis

On October 16, 1962, President John F. Kennedy received photographs of Soviet missile installations under construction in Cuba, only 90 miles (144.8 km) away from the United States. It looked as if the Soviet Union was preparing to launch a nuclear attack on the United States from Cuba. In a televised speech, President Kennedy made it clear that the United States took the threat seriously. For thirteen days, the two most powerful countries in the world were on the brink of war. Many communications went back and forth between the countries. The crisis finally ended on October 28, when Soviet leader Nikita Khrushchev promised to remove the missiles. In return, the United States promised not to invade the Soviets' ally, Cuba.

television. Then they celebrated by going out to eat at what had been a "whites only" restaurant. When they walked through the door, the other diners froze. They stared in amazement as the well-dressed African American family approached a waiter. After a few seconds of shocked silence, the waiter showed the Rices to a table.

Many things were about to change for the Rice family.

The Civil Rights Act of 1964 was designed to end discrimination in many areas, including voting and employment rights. President Johnson signed the act on July 2.

Discovering Her Dream

Condoleezza Rice loved to learn. She did so well in school that she was able to skip two grades (first and seventh). Condi had many different interests, including art, dance, music, and languages. It was hard for her to decide what she liked best. People often asked her what she wanted to be when she grew up.

"My answer would change from week to week," Condi recalls. "Most of the time I wanted to be a concert pianist."

A NEW LIFE

In 1967, when Condi was thirteen years old, her father accepted a position as an administrator at the University of Denver. The Rices left the hot climate of southern Alabama for the snowy mountains of Denver, Colorado. It was quite a change for the whole family. Condoleezza began tenth grade at St. Mary's Academy. For the first time, she attended an integrated school with both black and white students. Condi was one of only three black students in her class. Somehow, the Rices had given their daughter such confidence in herself that it never occurred to her to feel different from or inferior to the other students.

Competitive figure skating was a popular sport in Denver. Condi started taking lessons right away. She had to get up at 4:30 A.M. in order to get to the skating rink in time for her 5:00 A.M. lessons. John faithfully drove Condi back and forth every day. As an athlete himself, he loved to see his daughter involved in any type of sport. Angelena was not so sure. She worried that Condi would fall and hurt her hands. Then her piano career would be ruined.

A Trip to the White House

In the 1950s, there were very few opportunities for African Americans. Still, John and Angelena Rice taught their young daughter that she could grow up to do anything she wanted to do or be anything she wanted to be. One summer, the Rices took a family trip to the nation's capital, Washington, D.C. When they visited the White House, a photographer snapped a picture of ten-year-old Condi, standing in front of the gates. Gazing up at the president's mansion, Condi casually remarked, "I'm going to be in there one day." She could never have dreamed how true those words would be!

For a while, Condi thought she might want to be a professional figure skater. She continued taking lessons and competed with other skaters at the Denver Figure Skating Club. As time went on, the dream faded. Condi realized she did not have a talent for the sport.

"I worked very hard at it," she says, "but it was clear from the way I skated that I would never be an Olympic champion." Reluctantly, Condi gave up skating and started concentrating on the piano again.

A SUBTLE FORM OF RACISM

One day, Condi met with her high school guidance counselor to discuss the results of her SAT test. The challenging exam is often used to determine whether students are prepared to enter college. For some reason, Condi had not received a very good score on the test. The guidance counselor informed her that she was not "college

As she did with many of her interests, Condi approached ice skating with great determination.

material" and suggested that she should get a job after high school instead of pursuing higher education.

Condi was stunned. She earned straight A's on her report cards. She took advanced classes in every subject, including Latin and French. She played on the tennis team, studied classical piano, and competed in figure skating. On top of everything else, Condi was two years ahead of all the other students in her class. She knew that she was "college material."

The guidance counselor had not bothered to look at Condi's school records. All she saw was a young black girl with a low test score. "I think it was a subtle form of racism," Condi says. "It's the problem of low expectations [for African Americans]."

Thankfully, Condi had supportive parents who told her to disregard the counselor's advice. In 1969, at the age of fifteen, Condoleezza Rice graduated from high school. She immediately enrolled in the University of Denver. As always, Condi excelled in school. Even as a freshman, she made her mark. On one occasion, she challenged a professor in front of 250 other students in a crowded lecture hall.

The professor was explaining the racist teachings of physicist William Shockley. Shockley believed that white people were genetically superior to black people. Their physical, chemical, and biological makeup made them naturally more intelligent than blacks. Blacks were born less intelligent and were not capable of being educated to the same extent as whites. Condi's professor went on and on, explaining these ridiculous theories as if they were true. The other students might have accepted this nonsense, but Condi knew better. She stood up to the professor and contradicted him.

"You really shouldn't be presenting this as fact, because there's plenty of evidence to the contrary," she said. When the professor argued with her, Condi said, "I'm the one who speaks French here. I'm the one who plays Beethoven. I'm better at your culture than you are! Obviously, these things can be taught. It doesn't have anything to do with whether or not you are black." She got an A in the class.

Like her parents, Condoleezza refused to accept the limitations others tried to place on her. She was determined to succeed in school, and she did.

A BRAND NEW DREAM

Going into her second year of college, Condi was working toward a degree in music. She had been preparing for a career as a concert pianist since she was three years old. But in her sophomore year, Rice had an eye-opening experience. "I went to a music festival

Despite the negative comments of her high school guidance counselor, Condi excelled at college. This photograph shows Condi standing with her parents after receiving an award.

camp and met kids who could play from sight what it had taken me all year to learn!" she exclaims. "Technically I could play almost anything. But I realized I'd never play it the way great pianists do."

Condi was good, but not good enough to have a successful career in music. "Mozart never had to practice," she observes. "I was going to have to practice and practice and practice—and still never be extraordinary." People who have degrees in music usually become one of two things: professional musicians or music teachers. Condi knew she would never make it as a concert pianist. "Oh my goodness!" she thought. "I'm going to end up teaching thirteen-year-olds to murder Beethoven!" She did not want to be a music teacher at all.

It was really disappointing for Condi, to discover that her dreams of being a musician would not come true. But she took it all in stride. "I don't do life crises," she says. "I really don't. Life is too short. Get over it. Move on to the next thing!"

Then in her third year of college, Rice had to change her major. She needed to get her degree in something other than music. Condi took a class on international politics. She started learning about different forms of government around the world. She learned how governments from different countries worked together and against each other. Dr. Josef Korbel taught the class. Korbel had been a diplomat in Czechoslovakia. During World War II, he escaped from the Nazis and went to England. After the war, he and his family returned to Czechoslovakia. When a communist government took over the country, the Korbels escaped a second time, this time to the United States. Josef Korbel was then an expert on Soviet affairs.

One day, Korbel gave a lecture on Soviet leader Joseph Stalin. Condi was fascinated by the class. "It was love at first sight!" she says. Rice wanted to know more about Russia, its history, and its culture. She wanted to understand its government and its people. She wanted to learn its language. Condi had discovered a brand-new dream. She shocked her friends and family by announcing that she would earn her degree in Russian history.

Rice wasn't exactly sure what sort of career she would have as an expert in Russian affairs. But Korbel believed Condoleezza had a rare gift for understanding and applying the principles of political science. He urged her to pursue her studies with a passion. "I loved his course and I loved him," Rice says. She refers to Korbel as "one of the most influential figures in my life, next to my parents."

In 1974, Rice graduated from the University of Denver *cum laude*, which means "with honors." She was only nineteen years old.

The Soviet Union

From 1917 to 1991, fifteen Eastern European countries joined together to form one nation—the Soviet Union. Because the largest and most powerful of these countries was Russia, people sometimes used both "Russian" and "Soviet" to refer to the nation. Today, the Soviet Union no longer exists; the fifteen countries govern themselves separately. Some people refer to the Eastern European region as "the former Soviet Union."

Condi graduated from the University of Denver in 1974 and headed to University of Notre Dame for graduate school.

The following year, Rice earned her master's degree from the University of Notre Dame. She thought briefly about going on to law school, but Korbel wouldn't hear of it. He convinced her to come back to the University of Denver and enroll in his new graduate program to study international relations.

"You are very talented," he told Rice. "You have to become a professor."

In 1981, Rice earned her doctorate, a Ph.D. in political science, and accepted a teaching position at the prestigious Stanford University, not bad for the girl who was told she was "not college material." Great things were in store for Dr. Condoleezza Rice.

Madeleine Korbel Albright

Condoleezza Rice was one of Josef Korbel's favorite students. Rice often spent time at the Korbel home, where she met the professor's daughter, Madeleine. The two women shared a love of Russian politics. Both women spent hours listening to Dr. Korbel's lectures, discussions, and debates. Both would become experts in Soviet politics. And one day, both women would hold cabinet-level positions in the White House. Madeleine got there first. In 1996, President Clinton appointed her as the first female secretary of state. Madeleine Korbel Albright became the highest-ranking woman in the history of the United States government.

This is an aerial photograph of Stanford University. The tower on the left side is part of the Hoover Institution on War, Revolution, and Peace, which was founded by Herbert Hoover, a U.S. president and graduate of Stanford.

Professor Rice at Stanford

In 1981, Condoleezza Rice moved to California to begin teaching political science at Stanford University. In political science classes, students learn the basic principles and conduct of governments around the world. At twenty-six years old, Rice was not much older than her students. She had to be careful to maintain a professional atmosphere in the classroom. Rice wanted her students to know that she cared about them. Having been in college recently herself, she understood what their lives were like, but she never let the students forget that she was the teacher.

A STEEL MAGNOLIA

One of the other professors noted that Rice had "tremendous ability and intelligence—the maturity of someone far beyond her age." Another professor described Rice as a "steel magnolia." He explained that she had all the charm and grace for which southern ladies are famous. She appeared delicate and beautiful, like a magnolia flower. But underneath, Rice was strong and tough. She wouldn't let other people run over her. She didn't collapse or wilt under pressure.

Rice became a very popular professor on the Stanford campus. Students lined up to enroll in her classes. Rice remembered the struggles she faced in college, as she tried to discover what course of study to pursue. Now she advised her young students: "Find your passion. You've got four years in college, and if at the end of it you know what makes you want to get up in the morning, that's all you need."

She told their parents, "Don't panic if your kid comes home and says, 'I'm going to major in Etruscan Art.' Who knows? Maybe they'll manage to turn that into something they can actually make a living from. You're never really fulfilled unless you find something you love to do." That fulfillment was something Rice experienced herself on a daily basis.

In 1984, Professor Rice was given the Walter J. Gores Award, Stanford's highest award for excellence in teaching. She had become actively involved in all aspects of university life. Rice supported the Stanford Cardinal sports teams. She was a big fan of both men's and women's basketball, and, of course, football. On the weekends, she even traveled to other cities to attend away games. Rice continued to play the piano as an outlet for her own creative expression. Sometimes she gave concerts on the campus. In addition to being a professor, Rice was also a fellow at the Center for International Security and Arms Control. A fellow is a student who takes advanced courses in a highly specialized study program.

As time passed, Rice developed a reputation for her expertise in Soviet politics. Democratic Congressman Gary Hart decided to run for president of the United States. He knew that he would have to make speeches about how he thought the United States should work with the governments of other countries. He asked Rice to give him foreign policy advice during his campaign.

While she was teaching at Stanford, Rice wrote her first book, *Uncertain Allegiance: The Soviet Union and the Czechoslovak Army*. She dedicated the book to her parents and to Dr. Josef Korbel "in memory of his love for Czechoslovakia."

LOST AND FOUND

Rice's earliest childhood memories were of Sunday school, choir practice, and youth fellowship. As a minister's daughter, Rice says the church had always been a very important part of her life. But now that she was an adult, living on her own and pursuing a challenging career, Rice found it difficult to maintain regular church attendance. She simply got too busy. "Maybe I had to work. Maybe I had to do something about a lecture I had to give on Monday. I was always traveling . . . and when I got home, I was just too tired to go to church," Rice recalls.

Slowly but surely, the faith that had been so precious to her seemed to slip farther and farther away. Rice says it was still there, but "not front and center in the way that I lived my life daily."

One Sunday morning, Rice was shopping at the grocery store. She struck up a conversation with a man buying supplies for a church picnic. Suddenly he asked Rice, "Do you play the piano?" The church down the

The Cold War

After World War II, the United States and the Soviet Union were the two most powerful countries in the world. They were also enemies. The countries disagreed on many important issues of government and economics. At times, it seemed likely that the two superpowers would end up at war. (A superpower is an extremely powerful nation that has great influence over other countries and world affairs.) From the 1940s through the 1980s, these nations did engage in a "cold war." There were no actual battles fought, but there were plenty of threats made, minor conflicts, and acts of hostility. The United States objected to the Soviet takeover of other Eastern European countries. Soviet leaders claimed that "capitalist" governments like the one that ran the United States were responsible for World War II. There were dangerous moments during the Cuban Missile Crisis in 1962 and the Soviet invasion of Czechoslovakia in 1968. Both the United States and the Soviet Union constantly stockpiled weapons and built up their militaries to prepare for the possibility of war. At times, the whole world was tense and anxious, waiting to see what would happen.

street desperately needed a pianist for their weekly services. Before she knew it, Rice had agreed to play for them.

"As a result of going there and playing and getting involved again with the church community, I began to see how much of my faith . . . I'd taken for granted." A moving sermon stirred Rice's heart. She felt as if God was speaking directly to her, challenging her to take her faith in him more seriously. Rice says, "You know, it's a good thing that I did, because I was soon to learn why faith is so important in your daily life."

A SAD GOOD-BYE

When Rice was in high school, her mother had been diagnosed with breast cancer. Many people who have cancer die within a few years—or even months—of their diagnosis. Rice had much more time to be with her mother. Angelena bravely fought the disease for fifteen years. But in 1985, she lost the battle. Angelena died at the age of sixty-one. Rice was heartbroken to lose her mother like this. They had been so close. Yet she realized that she could be thankful Angelena had hung on so long. "I'm grateful she lived until I was thirty," Rice says.

Rice went home to Colorado for the funeral. After the service, a few close friends and relatives made their way to the Rice family home. Calmly and graciously—as her mother had taught her to be, Rice led everyone in a simple prayer of thanksgiving for Angelena's life. Then she sat down at the piano. "Let's play some of Mother's favorite hymns," she said. Later, Rice observed that she could not have gotten through losing her mother "without a strong and robust faith." She says her recently renewed faith gave her peace and hope in the midst of her grief.

When she returned to Stanford, Rice became a fellow at the prestigious Hoover Institute. The institute was a think tank, which is a type of a research organization whose members analyze problems and plan future developments in political, economic, and social areas. The members of the Hoover Institute are usually highly acclaimed scholars and political leaders. They seek "to recall the voice of experience against the making of war, . . . to recall man's endeavors to make and preserve peace, and to sustain for America the safeguards of the American way of life."

THE PATH TO POLITICS

Condoleezza Rice was becoming widely known as an expert on Soviet politics. As time went on, she began to get involved in U.S. politics too. Back in the 1950s, Rice's father had been prevented from registering to vote by members of the Democratic Party. They required black voters to take an eligibility test that no one could pass. (White voters were not required to take any test.) The clerks asked ridiculous questions, such as "Who was Thomas Jefferson's great grandmother?" or "How many windows are there in the courthouse?" John Rice was shown a jar full of jelly beans and told to guess how many were in it. A wrong answer meant he couldn't vote.

Later, John heard about a Republican in the registrar's office who would secretly register blacks to vote. John, Rice says, became "the first Republican I knew. The Democrats would not register him to vote; the

Republicans did. My father has never forgotten that day, and neither have I."

Still, when Rice voted in her first election in 1976, she chose Democratic candidate Jimmy Carter. It wasn't long before she felt she had made a mistake. President Carter's foreign policy was weak. He admitted that he didn't know much of the history and politics of the Soviet Union. He seemed surprised when the communist nation invaded Afghanistan and took over the country by force. As an expert on Soviet affairs, Rice understood the very real threat posed by the Soviet Union during the Cold War. She believed the United States could not afford to underestimate its greatest enemy. The danger was just too great.

In 1980, Rice voted for the Republican candidate, Ronald Reagan. She felt much more comfortable with his strong stand against communism and the Soviet Union. President Reagan believed that having a prepared and powerful military was the best way to keep the peace. The Soviets were much less likely to start a war with the United States if there was good chance they would lose.

In some ways, Rice's personal beliefs were more in line with those of the Democratic Party. But when it came to international relations and foreign policy, she found herself fully supporting the Republican positions.

In 1984, Rice watched presidential candidate Walter Mondale give a speech to the Democratic National Convention. Over and over, Mondale referred to the need to assist "women, minorities, and the poor." It seemed to Rice as if Democrats viewed women and African Americans as helpless members of society to be pitied and protected. This irritated Rice so much that she decided to leave the Democratic Party for good. "I'd rather be ignored than patronized," she said.

Brent Scowcroft (right) would become the national security advisor to President George H. W. Bush.

As a professor at Stanford, Rice attended a dinner party for arms control experts. There she met Brent Scowcroft. Years earlier, Scowcroft had been the national security advisor for President Gerald Ford. Scowcroft was very impressed with Condoleezza Rice. He described her as "a young slip of a girl"—the youngest person at the dinner party. She was also the only woman and the only African American. She carried herself with grace, poise, and confidence. Rice asked Scowcroft a "brilliant question" on international law. The former security advisor says he was "absolutely captivated" by this gifted young woman.

Scowcroft invited Rice to join him in Washington, D.C., working on nuclear strategic planning for the Council on Foreign Relations. It was an incredible honor to be asked. Though it would mean temporarily leaving Stanford and her teaching position at the university, Rice didn't hesitate and said yes.

Nuclear Weapons

During the Cold War, both the United States and the Soviet Union stockpiled great numbers of nuclear weapons. Nuclear weapons are explosive devices. They get their energy from a process that involves splitting the nucleus of an atom, one of the tiniest particles of matter. Nuclear bombs are incredibly destructive. It only takes one to wipe out an entire city. In their race to keep up with each other, the world's superpowers had built enough nuclear bombs to destroy the entire planet several times. People everywhere were terrified about the idea of a nuclear war. They began to call for "arms control," a voluntary agreement between nations to limit the number and types of bombs they would produce.

At her first job in Washington, D.C., Rice worked in the Pentagon building.

Working in Washington

After five years of teaching political science at Stanford University, Rice was ready for a change. She eagerly accepted Brent Scowcroft's invitation to join the Council on Foreign Relations in Washington, D.C. The council was responsible for "nuclear strategic planning." Four members of the council shared one office in the Pentagon building. They worked under the supervision of Admiral William Crowe. The experts on the council helped military leaders plan effective strategies for dealing with the Soviet Union.

Because she knew so much about the communist country, Rice was able to explain how Soviet leaders thought and what they were likely to do in certain situations. Rice reported regularly to the joint chiefs of staff. This advisory body reports directly to the president of the United

States. It includes the chiefs of staff of the army and the air force, the commandant of the marine corps, and the chief of naval operations. In a way, Rice functioned as a teacher to the top men in the military. She was also a student. Her experiences in Washington taught her many new things. She saw a completely different side of the government and the military and how they work together.

"I gained so much respect for military officers and what they do," Rice says. "I really got an experience that few civilians have."

After two years on the council, Rice returned to teaching at Stanford University. She wrote her second book, *The Gorbachev Era*, with Alexander Dallin. This book was a collection of essays written by foreign policy experts. The experts discussed the political views of the new

Mikhail Gorbachev

In 1985, Mikhail Gorbachev was elected general secretary of the Communist Party of the Soviet Union. He also served as president of the Soviet Union from 1990 to 1991. Gorbachev was one of the country's most influential leaders. He brought much-needed reform to the troubled nation. Gorbachev urged Communist Party leaders to open up to new ideas in government, politics, and economics. He sought to build positive and constructive relationships with other countries. He paved the way for freedom and democracy in the Soviet Union. In recognition of his efforts, Gorbachev received the 1990 Nobel Peace Prize.

Soviet leader and the way these views were reshaping the Soviet Union. Rice compiled all the essays, edited them, and added one of her own. The book was used as a study guide at college campuses around the country.

In 1988, the United States ambassador to the Soviet Union contacted Rice. The ambassador asked Rice to join him on a trip to Bulgaria. They would meet with Soviet diplomats and government officials to discuss arms control. Rice was thrilled to have the opportunity. The Soviets were impressed by her because she spoke fluently in Russian and understood so much of their history and culture.

BACK TO WASHINGTON

In 1990, Brent Scowcroft became the national security advisor once again. This time, he worked for the administration of President George H.W. Bush. One of the first things Scowcroft did was invite Condoleezza Rice to join his new staff. Rice would be working in the White House for the National Security Council. She was appointed to be director of Soviet and East European Affairs.

Rice remembers her first meeting with the president in the Oval Office. Just being in the room itself was an awe-inspiring experience. "It was amazing!" she says. "I was completely overwhelmed. Anybody who tells you that they're not overwhelmed the first time they walk into the Oval Office is lying to you, because you walk in there and there's all that history. . . ."

As a child, Rice had casually remarked that she would be in the White House one day. She admits that she had no idea what she meant when she said it. Rice certainly never dreamed that she would work there as one of the president's top advisors.

In her new position, Rice closely followed world news and events as they unfolded. She carefully analyzed what had happened and why. She considered how these events would affect the United States and other countries. She formed opinions as to how the United States should respond to the events. Then Rice met with President Bush and presented all of her information to him. This helped the president make key decisions and create important national policies.

President Bush scheduled a series of summit meetings with Soviet President Mikhail Gorbachev and other heads of state. They needed to discuss ways to develop greater cooperation between the two superpowers on global issues such as arms control and expansion of trade. They would

Rice discusses matters of foreign policy with President Bush (right) and other White House officials as part of her work for the National Security Council.

also talk about the growth of freedom and democracy in the Soviet Union and around the world. It was Rice's job to coach the president and help him prepare for these crucial meetings. She gave him all the strategies, statistics, and background information he needed to communicate with the Soviet leaders. Then Rice sat in on the actual meetings and took notes. She analyzed what had taken place that day: what had been accomplished and what still needed to be accomplished. Rice suggested additional ways the president might make progress in his talks with Soviet officials.

At the end of the day, Rice was one of a handful of senior aides who were invited to attend the exclusive dinner meetings. It showed how much the president respected and appreciated her work. Speaking of Rice, President Bush once said to Gorbachev, "She tells me everything I know about the Soviet Union."

AT THE WHITE HOUSE

Rice got to know President Bush and his wife Barbara very well, and they became close friends. Many other White House staffers admired Rice. Not only was this young woman incredibly gifted, she was also diligent and disciplined. She worked hard and gave everything her best effort. It seemed that Rice was always polite and gracious, never rude or argumentative. Yet she knew when to stand firm.

Once, Rice was in a meeting at the White House with Boris Yeltsin, a rising leader in the Soviet government. Yeltsin was furious that Brent

Scowcroft had been sent to talk to him. He did not want to meet with the national security advisor. He wanted to meet with President Bush directly. Yeltsin tried to push past the office staff to leave the conference room in search of President Bush. Condoleezza Rice stood up and physically blocked the door. After a few minutes, Yeltsin calmed down and backed off.

Rice was working with some of the most powerful people in the world. She had privileges and responsibilities others would give anything to have. Rice had just turned thirty-seven. She was still considered very young for a person in her position at the White House. Most of her coworkers were at least twenty years older than she was, and most of them were white men. Rice stood out in every possible way. But Rice never got caught up in the power or prestige. While working at the

Rice talks with Boris Yeltsin. Yeltsin served as Russia's president from 1990 to 1999.

White House, she pitched in and helped wherever she was needed. In 1990, when Iraq invaded Kuwait, President Bush needed to issue a public response to the incident quickly. Another staff member had created a list of talking points for the president. He didn't have time to send it to a secretary, so he went to the computer to type it up himself. For a few seconds, Rice watched him "hunt and peck"—pressing one key at a time as he found the correct alphabet letter. Then she sat down and typed it for him.

Rice was amazed at how quickly she got used to her life in international politics. "I remember coming back from a trip to Moscow and getting a message from Brent Scowcroft," she says. "He wanted to know if I could come to the White House. He said, 'We're going to meet Gorbachev on Friday in Finland to talk about the Gulf War.' And I said

George H. W. Bush

George Herbert Walker Bush became the forty-first president of the United States in 1989. A former navy pilot and son of a U.S. senator, Bush had a long history of service to his country. He was elected to two terms in the U.S. House of Representatives. Later, he was appointed U.S. ambassador to China. Afterward, Bush became director of the Central Intelligence Agency (CIA). He then served two terms as vice president of the United States under President Ronald Reagan. During his own presidency, Bush led the United States and the United Nations to victory over Iraq in the Gulf War.

to myself, '*Another meeting?*' Then I thought, 'Listen to you! When you started this job, you would have given your right arm to meet with Gorbachev and now it's *another meeting?*'"

THE FALL OF THE SOVIET UNION

Condoleezza Rice had the ideal job for any expert in Soviet affairs. She had the privilege of being in the White House during one of the most significant events in modern history, the fall of the Soviet Union.

For many people, life under communism could be difficult. This photograph shows people waiting in line for bread.

For more than seventy years, the Soviet Union had been the most powerful communist country in the world. In the communist political system, the government owns all the land, buildings, and factories. It controls schools, businesses, and churches. Everyone works together for the good of the community. Then everyone shares in its success. However, this rarely happens. Instead, government leaders often take advantage of their authority to restrict the people's freedoms and confiscate their property. Some families would be told how many children they could have and what kind of work they must do. Some leaders become wealthy, while ordinary people suffer and fall into poverty. People are forbidden from questioning the actions of the government. Corrupt officials imprison and even execute those who dare to oppose them. It may be difficult to leave the country without permission.

In a quest for more power, communist countries have attacked and invaded neighboring countries, forcing them to adopt the communist way of life. After World War II, the Soviet Union took control of many Eastern European countries, including Albania, Bulgaria, Czechoslovakia, East Germany, Hungary, Poland, and Romania. After decades of abuse, the people of the Soviet Union grew tired of the oppressive communist rule. More people became convinced that communism was not an effective system of government.

In 1985, Mikhail Gorbachev began a series of government reforms he called *perestroika*, which means "restructuring." He challenged other leaders to welcome *glasnost*, or "openness and freedom in Russian politics." People responded to Gorbachev's leadership. Changes began taking place in communist countries all over Eastern Europe. For the first time in decades, these countries had elections in which people were allowed to vote for political candidates who were not members of the Communist Party. If the Communist Party members lost the elections—and

After the fall of the Soviet Union, people began taking down communist symbols, such as this statue of Vladimir Ilich Lenin, founder of the Russian Communist Party.

they did—they agreed to give up control peacefully. This had never happened before.

Gorbachev began negotiations with President Reagan to end the Cold War. Both the Soviet Union and the United States agreed to reduce their number of weapons and the size of their military forces. Some members of the Communist Party opposed the changes Gorbachev made. They tried to take back control of the Soviet Union, but they were unsuccessful. In 1991, the Soviet Union collapsed and dissolved into fifteen separate countries. Mikhail Gorbachev resigned his presidency. Boris Yeltsin took over the leadership of Russia, the largest of the fifteen new countries.

The world was stunned. The Soviet Union had seemed so powerful. Most people thought they would never live to see the day that communism was overthrown in Russia. Condoleezza Rice had a front-row seat.

"I felt such joy for the Russian people," she says. "I also felt amazement at how it happened. Everything I'd been taught as a political scientist had said 'the state will try to survive.' And this was a state with five million men under arms and 30,000 nuclear weapons. But on December 25, 1991, Gorbachev sat there on television and said, 'Never mind!'"

There were many more surprises in store for Rice.

FIVE

A New Challenge

Once again, Condoleezza Rice left Washington, D.C., and returned to teaching at Stanford University. She was ready for a break from the intense pressure of her work at the White House. Some people couldn't understand how Rice could walk away from such a powerful and important position.

"I like balance in my life," Rice explained to a reporter. "I wanted a life. These [political] jobs are all-consuming. I have what is a blessedly normal life here. I like going to the cleaners and the coffee shop on Saturday morning."

When Senator Pete Wilson was elected governor of California, he left a vacant seat in the Senate. There were people who thought Rice should run for office as his replacement. Rice did not have any interest in becoming a senator. She had declined to run for office before. Later on, Rice did accept an appointment from Governor Wilson. She served on the committee that reorganized California's legislative and congressional districts.

As an expert on Russian affairs, Rice contributed numerous articles to magazines and newspapers. Her work was published in *Time* magazine, *The Los Angeles Times*, and *The New York Times*. Reporters often asked her to talk about the fall of the Soviet Union. They interviewed her whenever they needed information on Russia or Eastern Europe for an upcoming report. Many respected businesses and organizations sought Rice's advice. They asked her to join their board of directors and help oversee their companies. Rice agreed to serve on the boards of Transamerica, Charles Schwab, Chevron, the International Advisory Council of J. P. Morgan, the University of Notre Dame, the San Francisco Symphony, the Carnegie Corporation, and the Hewlett Foundation. Chevron, a gas company, named an oil tanker after their newest board member—the U.S.S. *Condoleezza Rice*.

All this time, Rice continued teaching her popular classes in political science at Stanford. Rather than simply telling old "war stories" from her time in Washington, D.C., Rice challenged her students to participate actively in the learning process. As a part of their studies, they had to research, write, debate, and act out historical foreign policy decisions. Rice was honored with the School of Humanities and Sciences Dean's Award for Distinguished Teaching.

A STUNNING OFFER

In 1993, Rice received a call from Gerhard Casper, the president of Stanford University. Rice and Casper had always been on good terms and had a friendly working relationship. Rice thought Casper was calling to chat about plans for the upcoming school year. Instead, the university president made a startling announcement.

"Condi," he said, "I want you to be the next provost!"

The provost is the chief academic and budget officer of a university, the person responsible for managing the school's finances. It's the second most powerful position on campus. The provost answers only to the president. Normally, a provost works first as a professor, then as head of a

Rice speaks with Gerhard Casper, president of Stanford University, at an event.

department, then as a dean. He or she gradually rises to the top position among the university's faculty. Rice had never been a department head or a dean. She was only thirty-eight years old, still young for a professor at a prestigious school like Stanford University.

President Casper recalls Rice's initial response to his offer: "There was silence," he says. "You know, Condi is not someone who's easily stunned by anything, but there was absolute silence on the other end."

When she got over her shock, Rice was thrilled to accept the opportunity. She became the youngest provost in the 102-year history of the university. Rice was also Stanford's first female provost and she was Stanford's first African American provost. When the appointment was

Stanford University

Jane and Leland Stanford established Stanford University in memory of their fifteen-year-old son, Leland Jr., who died of typhoid fever. Since they could no longer do anything for their own child, they decided to use their wealth to do something for other people's children. The university opened its doors in 1891 to more than five hundred students.

Today, Stanford University educates more than fourteen thousand graduate and undergraduate students each year. In addition to the main school campus in California, there are nine international campuses. The university has created two dozen research centers and institutes. Stanford is known as one of the finest universities in the United States.

announced, most people were just as surprised as Rice had been. Some thought she should have accepted a smaller promotion, such as department head or dean, first. But President Casper was convinced that Rice would do an excellent job.

THE CHALLENGE

The year Condoleezza Rice became provost, Stanford had a more than $40 million budget deficit. In other words, the school had spent over $40 million more than it had coming in. In 1989, an earthquake had damaged more than two hundred buildings on the campus, each of which

Stanford University was facing a financial crisis when Rice became the provost.

had to be repaired or rebuilt. In addition, the school's expenses had grown because of rising costs for such things as employee health care. In spite of tuition payments, government grants, and private donations, the university had accumulated a tremendous amount of debt. It was an enormous problem. As the chief budget officer, Rice was responsible for coming up with a solution.

Rice had never managed such a huge budget before, but she believed she could handle it. She announced that her goal was to balance the budget within two years. Some people thought she was crazy, and others said it couldn't be done. The debts and deficits were too high. They thought Rice should accept the fact that Stanford would always have these problems.

Rice ignored this "conventional wisdom." She was determined to bring the university's finances under control. She gave the entire budget a complete and thorough overhaul. She started cutting services and laying off staff members. Suddenly, the once popular professor had some powerful enemies. People got angry about Rice's budget cuts. They didn't like losing jobs and programs. Faculty members complained that Rice made most of her decisions without consulting them. She didn't form committees or seek input from other staff members. The criticism intensified as time went on.

"I had to discipline the university not to spend more money than we were taking in. I had to make some tough calls," Rice remembers. "Students held a sit-in on the quad, decrying everything I was doing, because I had to lay off a very popular administrator."

Rice found no joy in firing people. "It's never pleasant. You feel bad for the dislocation it causes in people's lives," she says. "But I strongly believe that when you take a job, you also take the risk that you might not hold the job. When I had to lay people off, I eased the transition for them in any way I could. But sometimes you have to make difficult decisions and you have to make them stick. I think those were probably the toughest couple of years I went through. There were so many doubters."

Not everyone was against Provost Rice. There were many people who understood what she was trying to do and believed it was necessary. Even those who didn't agree with her respected Rice for her courage and leadership. They appreciated the fact that she was open and direct. She did not engage in gossip or backstabbing. There were no secret deals going on behind closed doors. Even in the midst

Rice participates in a commencement ceremony at Stanford University. No matter what difficulties or resistance she encountered, Rice remained calm and collected— a true professional.

of the most intense confrontations, Rice maintained a polite, professional demeanor. Someone said Rice had a "velvet-gloved forcefulness." Through it all, Rice kept focused on the goal of achieving a balanced budget.

AFFIRMATIVE ACTION

In addition to complaints about budget cuts, Rice often received criticism for not supporting affirmative action aggressively. Affirmative action is a policy that promotes giving opportunities to women and minorities to make up for discrimination that they had encountered in the past. People who support affirmative action believe universities should make an extra effort to hire women and minorities as faculty members. They feel that women and minority students should receive preferential treatment in the admissions and enrollment process to universities. Supporters say affirmative action is the only way to bring balance and diversity to college campuses and workplaces.

People who oppose affirmative action believe the policy is unfair. Universities end up hiring staff or accepting new students on the basis of their sex or skin color, rather than on their qualifications. More qualified candidates are denied jobs in favor of less qualified candidates who belong to a minority group. Opponents say affirmative action creates the same type of discrimination it seeks to remedy.

Rice admitted that there were times when she may have benefited from affirmative action. People who wanted diversity were looking to bring women and African Americans into their programs. Her race and gender may have been a consideration when she was given jobs or admission to schools. On the other hand, Rice had been raised by parents who insisted on personal excellence. Rice had worked hard for everything she achieved. She never got a job simply because she was an African American or a woman. Rice didn't think anyone else should, either.

To Rice, affirmative action policies almost seemed to imply that women and minorities were helpless victims. Universities needed to give these people special treatment because they weren't capable of meeting the same standards as everyone else. Rice could not support that view. In her position as provost, she did try to encourage diversity on the staff and in the student body. She wanted to give opportunities to women and minorities. Still, Rice was much more concerned about hiring people who were competent and qualified, regardless of their race or sex.

THE TRIUMPH

After two long, difficult years, Condoleezza Rice made an astonishing announcement: the budget had been balanced. Stanford no longer had a $40 million deficit. It had no deficit at all. In fact, the university was now $14.5 million ahead. That money had been set aside in a special fund to be used in emergencies or when unexpected expenses arose. No one could believe it. Rice had accomplished her goal. To this day,

Rice considers balancing Stanford's budget as her greatest achievement. "We were never in the red," she says proudly.

For six years, Rice served as provost of the university. She worked hard to reform and reorganize educational programs for undergraduates. She used creative problem-solving to help the university overcome challenges and take on new and exciting projects. She inspired students to discover their passion, just as she had at the University of Denver years before. In her free time, Rice continued to write for national and international publications. She completed her third book, *Germany Unified and Europe Transformed: A Study in Statecraft*, which she co-authored with Philip Zelikow.

Always a sports fan, Rice enthusiastically supported the Stanford Cardinal teams. One weekend, to celebrate her birthday, she attended a women's basketball game, a men's basketball game, and a football game. Then she watched the National Football League's San Francisco 49ers

Rice enjoys working out and is committed to physical fitness.

game on television. To maintain her own physical fitness, Rice kept up a rigorous training program with Stanford's football coach.

"Exercise is a high priority for me," she says. "I do some of my best thinking on the treadmill."

When she wasn't working or working out, Rice spent time with family and friends. Her father had remarried and moved to Palo Alto, California, not too far from where Rice lived. Though it had been years since she had worked at the White House, Rice still kept in touch with her friends and colleagues from Washington, D.C., including former President George H.W. Bush, his wife Barbara, and the rest of the Bush family. That special relationship would soon bring new changes to Rice's life.

SIX

Back to Washington

Rice first met George and Barbara Bush's oldest son in 1995. George W. Bush was then a co-owner of the Texas Rangers baseball team. The two sports fans found plenty of things to talk about. But when they met again in 1998, the topic of conversation was anything but sports. George W. Bush had been elected governor of Texas. Now Governor Bush was considering running for president of the United States. His parents suggested he meet with Rice to discuss foreign policy issues.

Rice and Bush hit it off right away. They shared the same concerns about America's strengths and weaknesses. They both agreed that the country needed a stronger military and that U.S. soldiers should not be sent constantly on "police duty" in other countries all over the world.

The United States needed to actively strengthen its relationships with its allies. At the same time, the country needed to be firm and consistent in the way it dealt with its enemies. The more they talked, the more Bush and Rice liked each other. They discovered that they had many things in common. Each respected and appreciated the other person's point of view.

Rice was very impressed with Bush. "He has the kind of intellect that goes straight to the point. You can get a bunch of academics in a room and they can talk for three hours and never actually get to the point," she explains. "I have learned to admire people who challenge others to get to the point, and he's very much that way."

Not long after this meeting, Bush got right to the point in asking Rice to join his presidential campaign. A presidential candidate must explain to voters how he or she plans to lead the nation. The candidate should be able to express opinions on important world events. He or she will be asked to describe how he or she thinks the United States should interact with other countries. Bush wanted Rice to be his top foreign policy advisor. She would help him organize his thoughts and ideas about international politics. She would prepare him for the tough questions he would be asked in interviews and debates. In some ways, Rice would be Bush's tutor, filling him in on some aspects of world history and current events that he might not be aware of.

Rice decided that this was an opportunity that she couldn't pass up. She had already planned to take a "sabbatical," a year off from teaching, in order to devote some time to research and her ongoing study of international politics. She had told others, "If you're called upon by your country to do public service, it's your obligation to do so." In 1999, Rice resigned from her position as provost at Stanford University to hit the campaign trail with George W. Bush.

Many people at the university were sad to see her go, especially Gerhard Casper, the university's president. In a farewell address, Casper said, "Condi is the best collaborator I have ever had. During the last five years, she has not only been the university provost, but I have treated her as my deputy in every respect. She has fully deserved to be so treated. . . . Together we have tackled everything from undergraduate education reform to graduate housing. The ease with which we have communicated and collaborated is remarkable, given our seeming cultural differences— for instance, in the backgrounds of a black woman from segregated Birmingham, Alabama, and a white man from war-torn Hamburg, Germany. Condi and I have become close friends. . . ." President Casper told Rice that she had "shown a deep love of learning" and had "helped the university to build structures to help others undergo the transforming experience of education." He presented Rice with a special gift: a rare first-edition Russian language copy of the novel *War and Peace*, which had been printed in 1868.

Rice didn't know whether she would be returning to Stanford after the national elections. She decided to keep her campus condominium and her season tickets to the Cardinal's basketball games, but she was ready for a new adventure.

THE CAMPAIGN

As the 2000 presidential campaign began, Rice found herself in a whirl-wind of activity. She had lengthy meetings with Bush on a daily basis. She worked with other aides and foreign policy team members to stay on top of the latest news and world events. They examined every aspect of international politics. They helped the governor create guidelines and policies for the government's future relationships with other countries.

Rice helped keep presidential hopeful George W. Bush up-to-date on foreign relations issues on the campaign trail.

Foreign policy is a very complicated subject. The governor needed to show the American people that he had a good plan. He had to be able to explain this plan clearly and convincingly in campaign speeches and television interviews.

With all of her expertise in this area, Rice played a major role in the Bush campaign. Bush said that she was the person who could "explain to me foreign policy matters in a way I can understand." He added, "She's both a good manager and an honest broker of ideas . . . She's a close confidante and a good soul."

During the presidential campaign, staffers worked hard to reach voters with information about Governor Bush and his platform. Rice was one of several top aides who appeared regularly on television news and talk shows, discussing the governor's views and his qualifications for the presidency. Sometimes an election can get ugly. Candidates say unkind, and even untrue, things about each other. Politicians seize on each others' mistakes and use them as examples of why the opponent is not fit for office. Their aides and assistants do the same. Intense media coverage can make a misspoken word national news. Rice kept tight control over the people who were part of the team of advisors. She didn't want them to make any embarrassing mistakes that would reflect badly on Governor Bush.

A reporter asked Rice if it was true that no one on the foreign policy team was allowed to speak to the media without her permission. "You make me sound like a tyrant!" she replied. Then Rice smiled. "We *are* disciplined," she said. "We *are* disciplined."

Rice impressed many people with her speech at the Republican National Convention in 2000.

Rice made headlines herself when she gave a stirring speech at the Republican National Convention. People who had never heard of Rice were amazed by her speech. She had such poise and depth. She was so articulate. Everyone started talking about this "rising star" in the Republican Party.

A GREAT BOSS

Rice couldn't have been happier working for George W. Bush. "He's really smart—and he's also disciplined, which I admire," she said. "He's tough, calm, and even-keeled. Any campaign has its ups and downs, and if you follow the perturbation [anxiousness and confusion], you'll drive yourself crazy—but he never does. He says, 'We've got a good strategy, we're staying on course.' He also has a great sense of humor."

Rice also had a lot of respect for the way Governor Bush interacted with the rest of his family. "I tremendously admire his relationship with his wife, Laura. It's beautiful, so tender and supportive. And I love his relationship with his daughters, because I had a great relationship with my father and there's nothing like that!" Rice has said. "I also admire his relationship with his parents. I love the fact that family and God mean so much to him."

A presidential campaign is nonstop, high-pressure, exhausting work. Things are happening twenty-four hours a day, seven days a week. At one point, Rice realized that she needed to take a few days off for rest and relaxation. She spent a week in Utah at a music camp, where she and the other students played the piano "twelve hours a day." Though she had decided against being a concert pianist, she still loved music and enjoyed having an outlet for creative expression. To Rice, the music camp was a refreshing break from the rigors of the campaign trail. She came back rested and ready to work.

A few months before the election, Rice relaxes with President Bush (middle) and Paul Wolfowitz (right), the future deputy secretary of defense, at Bush's ranch in Crawford, Texas.

A Close Election

The 2000 presidential election was one of the closest races in U.S. history. On November 7, Republican Governor George W. Bush narrowly defeated Democratic Vice President Al Gore, with an electoral vote of 271 to 267. Florida's twenty-five electoral votes had made the difference for Bush. But there were all kinds of complaints from Democrats and Republicans about voting irregularities in Florida and several other states. There were confusing ballots, missing ballots, and improperly counted ballots.

Vice President Gore wanted a recount in Florida. The recount confirmed that Bush had won by a handful of votes. Then both parties went to court over further recounts in a battle that raged on for thirty-five days. Finally, on December 13, Gore conceded the election to Bush.

CALLED TO SERVE

The Republican campaign was successful. George W. Bush was elected as the forty-third president of the United States. Governor Bush immediately began calling on his close friends and advisors to fill important government positions. He surrounded himself with the brightest and the best. Many of the people Bush chose to work with had served in similar positions during his father's administration. To George W. Bush, that meant that these were people he could trust. One of them was Condoleezza Rice.

On December 18, 2000, President-Elect Bush announced that he had asked Rice to be his new national security advisor. No woman had ever held this top-level position. It was an incredible honor. The national security advisor sits in an office just down the hall from the president at the White House. He or she is responsible for providing the president with all the information he needs to make decisions of international significance.

Former National Security Advisor Brent Scowcroft thought Rice was an excellent choice. "I think she will do a great job," he said. "She has the personality for it. She has the background for it. She starts off with a very powerful set of credentials."

John and Angelena Rice had taken Condoleezza on her first trip to the White House when she was ten years old. They had driven all the way from Birmingham to Washington, D.C. Each night, they stopped by the side of the road and slept in the car because there were no hotels that would allow African Americans to stay in their rooms. Now the Rices' "Little Star" would be working in the White House as one of the

President Bush announces his top three White House aides to the press, including Rice's appointment to the position of national security advisor.

This photograph shows Rice with her father a few years before his death.

top advisors to the president of the United States.

"I'm honored to have the chance," Rice said. "It's a remarkable thing. We're only what—140 years out of slavery?" Earlier in Birmingham, the Rices had been right. The United States did get better. There were all kinds of opportunities for African Americans now. And Condoleezza Rice was leading the way.

Unfortunately, Angelena didn't live to see her daughter named national security advisor. John did, but just barely. He had been suffering from heart disease and was in a terribly weakened state. He couldn't attend the press conference at the White House. But as he watched the announcement on television, his eyes filled with tears. Friends called to congratulate him. His second wife, Clara, held the phone up to his ear so he could listen, even if he couldn't talk back. A week later, John passed away.

When Rice officially accepted the appointment, President George W. Bush introduced her to the country by saying, "Dr. Rice is not only a brilliant person; she is an experienced person. She is a good manager. I trust her judgment. America will find that she is a wise person." Turning to Rice, he added, "I'm so honored that you're joining this administration."

ON THE JOB

Some political experts wondered how Rice would fit in at the White House. She was certainly qualified for the position. Clearly, President Bush had confidence in her. The other members of his staff were some of the most experienced and accomplished men in the nation. Many of them had begun their political careers when Rice was a child. They had served on the staff of two or three different presidents. In a meeting with men like Vice President Dick Cheney, General Colin Powell, and Donald Rumsfeld, would Rice be able to make her voice heard?

The answer was a resounding "yes." Rice was not intimidated by these political giants. She knew some of them quite well. Vice President Cheney first met Rice when she worked for the former President Bush. He was impressed by her knowledge and insight back then. "She knew more about the Soviet military than anyone I'd met," Cheney told a reporter.

General Powell's wife grew up in Birmingham, Alabama. Alma Powell knew the Rice family well. During the campaign and election process, the Powells often invited Rice to their home for dinner. It became such a regular occurrence that whenever Rice showed up for a visit, General Powell would call out, "Alma, Condi's home!" He told members of the media that Rice was like a daughter to him. "Condi was raised first and foremost to be a lady," Powell said. "She was raised . . . to be a person of great self-confidence in Birmingham, where there was no reason to have self-confidence because you were a tenth-class citizen and you were black. "

Other members of the president's staff quickly learned that Rice knew what she was doing. She spoke with authority. She carried herself with class. Rice took on every new challenge with diligence and determination. She exercised sound judgment. She had keen insights and observations. Rice also had the president's ear. He listened to her advice,

Rice enjoys a playful moment with Colin Powell in the Oval Office at the White House.

Like Father, Like Son

When George W. Bush was sworn in as the forty-third president of the United States, his father, the forty-first president, stood nearby watching proudly, wiping tears from his eyes. The Bushes became the second pair of father and son presidents in U.S. history. John Adams and his son, John Quincy Adams, were the first. Like the elder George Bush, John Adams served two terms as vice president. Then he succeeded George Washington to become the second president of the United States. John Quincy Adams became the country's sixth president in 1825. Abigail Adams and Barbara Bush are the only two women in history to have been both the wife and the mother of a U.S. president.

and not just on matters of national security. Rice was the only member of the president's staff who regularly vacationed with him and his family. When George and Laura Bush spent the weekend at the presidential retreat at Camp David, they often invited Rice to join them.

As national security advisor, Rice gets to meet with many foreign officials, such as Vladimir Putin, the president of Russia.

SEVEN

The War on Terror

O n most days, Rice would be the first person to meet with the president in the morning. She would give him brief updates on world news and events. These events might include army troop movements in Iraq, an election in France, or the latest report on the outbreak of AIDS in Africa. Together, Rice and Bush would discuss the appropriate American response. Rice once told a reporter, "As an advisor to the president, my job is to faithfully represent the views of the different agencies that make up the National Security Council and to organize the decision-making process so that the president can come to a conclusion about what he thinks."

Rice would travel frequently with the president as he met with heads of state from other countries. She would explain the president's international policies to reporters in press conferences and interviews and on television programs.

The new president and his security advisor faced their first real test when a U.S. military airplane was forced to make an emergency landing in China. The Chinese government insisted that the Americans had invaded their airspace and forced one of their fighter jets into a midair collision. They refused to give the damaged American aircraft permission to land, and when it did anyway, they seized the airplane and the crew and held them prisoner.

The U.S. government insisted that the airplane was clearly in international airspace and could prove it. Furthermore, the U.S. pilot said that the Chinese fighter pilot attacked him. With his airplane severely damaged, he had no choice but to land immediately, wherever he could. The airplane contained very sensitive information and equipment that the Chinese could steal and use against the United States. The U.S. government demanded that China return it at once.

The situation could have been disastrous. Since the fall of the Soviet Union, China had become the world's most powerful communist country. It was trying to become the newest superpower. There were many tense and anxious moments on both sides of the Pacific Ocean. The whole world watched to see what would happen. Condoleezza Rice went to work quickly to help the president devise a diplomatic solution to the crisis. In time, the U.S. government was able to convince the Chinese to release the crew unharmed and to return the airplane. The Chinese dismantled the airplane and sent it back in pieces. The international community breathed a huge sigh of relief. No one knew then that the United States's greatest test was still to come.

SEPTEMBER 11, 2001

Words cannot begin to describe the unbelievable tragedy and devastation of that fateful day. At 8:45 A.M., an airplane hijacked by terrorists crashed into the north tower of the World Trade Center in New York City. Minutes later, another airplane hurtled into the south tower. Massive explosions ripped through multiple floors of both office buildings. As terrified employees scrambled to evacuate, miles away a third airplane slammed into the Pentagon building in Washington, D.C. Before it could reach its intended target, a fourth plane nose-dived into a field in Pennsylvania, killing everyone on board. Back in New York City, onlookers watched in horror, as one after another, the 110-story twin towers collapsed on top of rescue workers,

Ambulances race to the scene of the attack on the twin towers in New York City on September 11, 2001.

firefighters, police officers, and people who worked in the towers. In just a matter of seconds, before anyone really understood what was going on, thousands of lives had been lost.

The people of the United States were stunned. Nothing like this had ever happened in the history of the country, or even of the world. Politicians and leaders struggled to put the disaster into perspective. They compared it to such tragic and life-changing events as the assassination of President John F. Kennedy, the Cuban Missile Crisis, and the Oklahoma City bombing. Others insisted that this was comparable to the unprovoked attack by the Japanese on American troops in Pearl Harbor, Hawaii, during World War II. They called it "the Pearl Harbor of the

Heroes on Flight 93

The passengers on United Airlines Flight 93 were headed to San Francisco when hijackers overtook the airplane and steered it toward Washington, D.C. In a panic, those who had cellular telephones began calling their loved ones. Family members told them about the attacks that had just taken place at the World Trade Center and the Pentagon. The passengers realized that the hijackers intended to use their airplane to wreak even more destruction. It was all part of the terrorists' plot. A small group of passengers decided to rush the cockpit and force the airplane to crash in a field before it could reach the White House or any other American landmark. Their bravery and sacrifice saved countless lives.

twenty-first century," and a "new Day of Infamy." (*Infamy* describes an outrageous, criminal, or shameful act. In 1941, President Franklin Delano Roosevelt said the December 7 attack on Pearl Harbor was "a date which will live in infamy.") President George W. Bush called the terrorist attacks "acts of war." An entire generation of Americans would now be asking each other, "Where were you on September 11?"

CONDI'S EXPERIENCE

Television talk show host Oprah Winfrey asked Condoleezza Rice the same question in an interview that took place a few months after the attack.

Shortly after the attacks, Rice, Vice President Dick Cheney (far right), and members of the White House staff met inside the operations center at the White House. Cheney was on the phone with the president at the time this photograph was taken.

"I was at my desk in the White House at around 8:45, when my executive assistant came in and said a plane had hit the World Trade Center. I thought, 'What a strange accident!' I called the president in Florida and said, 'Mr. President, a plane hit the World Trade Center.' And he said, 'What a weird accident.' Around nine, after I went to a staff meeting, my assistant handed me a paper that said a second plane had hit the World Trade Center, and I thought, 'My God, this is a terrorist attack!'"

As the national security advisor, Rice leapt into action. "I went into the Situation Room and began trying to gather the National Security Council principals for a meeting. But Colin Powell was in Latin America. I remember thinking, 'Is he in danger?' Then I turned to see a television report of a plane hitting the Pentagon. There was also a false report that a car bomb had gone off at the State Department. Moments later someone came up and said, 'Get to the bunker! The vice president is already there.'"

The White House has a special underground bunker, or hiding place, for the president and top government officials to use in times of extreme danger. The bunker is protected by advanced security systems and stocked with emergency supplies and communication devices.

"Before I left, I talked to the president again about whether or not he would come back to the White House," Rice says. "We didn't want him to, because Washington was under attack. When I got to the bunker, it occurred to me to call my aunt and uncle in Birmingham and say, 'Tell everybody I'm okay.' Then I began calling other governments to make sure they knew that the United States government was up and running."

Rice began to gather information about how many airplanes had already taken off from U.S. airports that morning and where they were supposed to be headed. All other airplanes would be ordered to stay on the ground until further notice. At least twenty-two airplanes were unaccounted for—air traffic controllers couldn't say for sure where they were. This was terrifying news. Rice explains, "We could imagine planes coming down all over the place. We know now that the plane that went down in Pennsylvania was probably headed either for the White House or the Capitol Building."

Later, it was learned that the attacks were carried out by members of a terrorist organization called al Qaeda. This group had previously carried out other attacks on Americans overseas. They had bombed U.S. embassies and battleships. No one ever thought that they would be so bold as to launch an attack on U.S. soil, or that they would be successful. People called September 11 a "wake-up call." For years, other nations had experienced terrorism. They prepared for it as best they could. These countries had all kinds of strict security regulations in place. They placed tight restrictions on certain types of activity and movement among their citizens. But Americans have always prized individual freedom and personal privacy. The citizens of the United States refuse to allow what they see as government interference in their daily lives. The terrorists took advantage of the freedom in the United States. Many of them came into the country legally and studied at American schools to learn how to fly the airplanes they intended to hijack.

"The very openness that we have to protect as Americans was turned against us," Rice says. "That was hard to deal with."

TAKING ON THE TERRORISTS

In a stirring speech, President Bush declared a war on terror. He called for swift action against the terrorist organizations responsible for the attacks. He promised to deal harshly with individuals and countries that sponsored terrorism by providing terrorists with financial support. Bush asked U.S. allies to join him in a worldwide effort to hunt down and destroy all terrorist operations, wherever they might find them. Otherwise, Bush warned, future terrorist attacks would be even more destructive.

The al Qaeda terrorist network had many bases in the country of Afghanistan. Osama bin Laden, the leader of al Qaeda, worked closely with the country's ruling political party, the Taliban. Taliban leaders hated western countries. They openly encouraged and supported terrorism.

For many years, the Taliban had imposed strict laws on the people of

Afghanistan. They banned all kinds of modern technology. They closed down churches and businesses. They prohibited the schooling of girls over the age of eight and closed Kabul University. The Taliban drove the people into poverty and starvation. Men and boys were forced to serve in the army or in terrorist training camps. Women were not allowed to go to school or work outside the home. In fact, they could not go out in public at all, unless they were covered from head to toe in heavy veils called *burkahs*. Anyone who broke the law, refused to follow the religious teachings of the Taliban, or spoke out against the government was tortured, and many were executed.

The United States and its allies decided to launch the first attack in the War on Terror in Afghanistan. The goal was to destroy Osama bin Laden and his network. American bombs wiped out the terrorist training camps and military bases. They also destroyed most of al Qaeda's communication systems, weapons, and supplies. The Taliban government was overthrown. Many of its leaders were arrested or killed. World leaders tried to help the people of Afghanistan establish a new democratic government.

Some people worried that this was not enough. "We're all concerned about another attack," Rice said. "All we can do is work as fast and furiously as we can to root out terrorists where they are, which is Afghanistan. I'd like to think that at the end of this, we will have conducted this campaign in a way that shows American strength and resolve, but also American humanity. And I would hope that life is going to be better for the Afghan people, too." For years, the people of Afghanistan had suffered under the harsh rule of the Taliban. The United States sent millions of dollars in food, clothing, and medical supplies to assist them in rebuilding their lives.

As the situation in Afghanistan came under control, the United States turned its attention to other countries and individuals involved in terrorism. In her role as U.S. national security advisor, Rice stayed in close contact with world leaders and heads of state. She kept them informed about the actions the United States had taken and planned to take in the future. She also appeared on numerous television programs, including *Face the Nation*, *60 Minutes*, *Larry King Live*, and *Meet the Press*. On these programs, Rice explained to the American people what was happening in the War on Terror. She shared what President Bush believed the United States should do to combat terrorism in the future.

Rice appears on television to discuss the War on Terror.

A TIME TO HEAL

Along with the president, Rice offered much-needed comfort and encouragement to the grieving nation. She worked hard to assure Americans that their government was doing everything possible to protect them and keep them safe. Someone asked Rice how she handled her own anxiety at a time like this.

"Since I was a little girl, I have relied on faith—a belief that I'm never alone, that the bottom will never fall out too far," she said. "That has always been a part of me, and I'm drawing on that now. I'm not a worrier. When I'm concerned about something, I figure out a plan of action, and then I give it to God. I just ask Him to carry me through it. God's never failed me yet."

In a speech on the National Day of Prayer, Rice went on to explain that strength can come "from many different sources, and it certainly comes from different sources for different people. But for many of us . . . it certainly relates to a deep and abiding faith in God, whatever one's religious background. For me it comes from a deep and abiding faith in Jesus Christ."

Rice's experiences as a professor also helped her cope with the crisis. "I think my time in academia prepared me more strongly than even I realized," she says. "I can't tell you how many times I taught decision simulations, in which I gave my students a crisis to deal with and then sat down with them afterward to go through the lessons. I learned things

This photograph shows one of the many candlelight vigils held across the United States to honor and remember those who lost their lives in the September 11 attacks.

like, 'The first reports are always wrong,' which I remember saying several times on September 11."

In the months that followed the terrorist attacks, the people of the United States rallied around the country. They held prayer vigils and memorial services. They raised money for the victims and their families. There was a renewed sense of patriotism. People hung American flags from their homes and businesses. They wore flag pins, ribbons, and T-shirts with messages that said, "God Bless America," "United We Stand," and "9-11-01: We Will Not Forget." Firefighters and police officers were honored as heroes for their bravery in service to the country.

Rice said, "The terrorists have got to be disappointed that the attack didn't bring America down—it brought us together."

Rice has become an internationally known political figure. She is shown here on al-Jazeera, a satellite television network based in Qatar.

EIGHT

"The Most Powerful Woman in the World"

Through the War on Terror, Condoleezza Rice had become one of the most visible members of the White House staff. She was interviewed for television, radio, and newspaper articles, and not just on matters of national security. Magazines such as *Vogue, Glamour,* and *Essence* featured Rice in photo spreads and personality profiles. Rice had both brains and beauty, and the world was taking notice. Even people who knew little about politics or international affairs recognized the face of Condoleezza Rice.

Because of her position of influence, some people called Rice "the most powerful woman in the world." She was the national security advisor during the greatest national security crisis in U.S. history. President Bush relied heavily on her insights and observations. He listened to her advice. Rice would end up having a tremendous impact on the country's future.

When Rice needed advice herself, she knew where to go. "I have good friends in foreign policy who are very, very smart," she says. "I've talked to Brent Scowcroft on occasion. I've talked to Brzezinski, Kissinger, and Sandy Berger. I also have two or three really close friends from my time at Stanford whom I talk to all the time. I try to draw on the wisdom of the American people through my relatives—I just try to keep a sense of how they're seeing things. And then, I'm a deeply religious person, so I turn to prayer frequently."

At the White House, Rice often works fourteen-hour days, six days a week. But on Sundays, she sets aside time for worship. She asks her assistants not to page her while she is in church. It isn't always easy, but Rice does whatever she can to make time for her family and friends. "Even in these busy times, I try to find time for the people who have meant a lot to me throughout my life," she says. "If you get caught up in the present and aren't somehow connected to those people, you can lose your way."

At forty-nine years old, Rice remains single. It isn't something she necessarily planned. In fact, she says she fully expected to get married and have children at some point. It just hasn't happened. Instead, she has experienced a rewarding career that has impacted thousands of lives in countries all over the world.

TIME OUT

When Rice needs to relax, she doesn't reach for a book. She says her parents enrolled her in way too many book clubs when she was a child so reading feels too much like work. Instead, Rice works out. "I love to exercise," she says. "Actually I don't love it while I'm doing it, but I love the feeling afterward. I also love to shop. I can get lost in a store for hours. I love malls." Of course, these days, Rice is usually accompanied by members of the Secret Service. These special bodyguards don't mind following her around. "They can handle shopping!" she jokes.

Ever her mother's daughter, Condoleezza Rice likes to look good. People in the press often comment on how her outfits and jewelry are always perfectly coordinated, just right for whatever occasion. Rice says she enjoys dressing well and admits to having a real weakness for shoes. Once in a great while, she experiences something that reminds her of the racism she came across as a child.

Recently at a department store, Rice asked a clerk to show her some gold earrings. The clerk kept directing Rice to the cheaper costume jewelry. "No," Rice said, "I really want to see the nicer jewelry." The clerk turned around and muttered something that sounded like "Black trash!"

Rice quickly replied, "Now let's get one thing clear. If you could afford anything in here, you wouldn't be working behind this counter. So I strongly suggest you do your job!"

Rice prefers not to make a big deal out of these incidents. "It's something that has probably happened to every black person at some point in time. In general, people who recognize me are respectful. They'll walk up and say, 'I saw you on TV and you're doing a nice job.' Or 'I don't really like what you're doing, but it's nice to meet you anyway.' I think you have a radar for when someone is reacting to you racially. But I think most of the time you give people the benefit of the doubt and assume that they're just having a bad day."

Rice refuses to see racism in every insult. She doesn't believe African Americans today should focus on the wounds of the past. "I would hope that we would spend our time thinking how to educate black children, particularly black children who are caught in poverty. I would hope that we would spend our time, as the president has said, 'turning back the soft bigotry of low expectations' against our children. Slavery is more than 150 years in the past, and yes, there's a continuing stain. I've often said slavery was America's birth defect. It was there from the beginning. But we have to turn now to the present and to the future. I'd rather be a minority in this country than in anyplace else in the world."

Rice believes it's possible that the United States will one day have an African American president. "Things in this country change very dramatically and very quickly," she says. "When you think that forty years ago in Birmingham, Alabama, we couldn't sit in the front of the bus or go into a restaurant. . . . Look at where we are now! It's a wonderfully adaptable country. We'll get there."

Some people have suggested that Rice herself should run for office. But over and over, Rice has insisted she has absolutely no interest in becoming president of the United States. She'd much rather be the commissioner of the NFL.

"I love football!" she exclaims. "I think the National Football League is a really terrific institution. I'd love to be associated with it someday."

Rice recently met the current commissioner, Paul Tagliabue, for the first time. Tagliabue told Rice that he had heard she was anxious to take

Condi in Concert

President and Mrs. Bush hosted a special ceremony at Constitution Hall to award famous Americans with National Medals of Arts and National Humanities Medals. Some of the nation's greatest doctors, educators, artists, dancers, and musicians had assembled to accept these awards. At the close of the ceremony, the national security advisor took the stage. Dressed in an elegant black ball gown, Rice sat at the piano and played a duet with world-famous cellist, Yo-Yo Ma. They performed the slow movement of Brahm's *Violin Sonata in D Minor.* Rice received a standing ovation from the crowd.

over his job. "Not to worry," she replied, "but let me know when you're thinking of retiring."

LOOKING TO THE FUTURE

When her time as national security advisor comes to an end, Rice thinks she may return to the university campus. "I'll probably go back to being an academic," she says. "I really love ideas and writing. I already have ideas for several books—none of which will be best-sellers. They'll be books on subjects such as the structure of American policy." Rice admits she probably would have written more already if she hadn't spent so much time watching football!

"I do love to teach and I miss my kids," Rice says. "In a class of twenty, there are always two or three for whom the lights go on. When that happens, I think I've done for them what Dr. Korbel did for me."

Rice's plans for the future certainly aren't set in stone. "I have learned to do what works for me—and that is to not look that far ahead; to do what you're doing, do it well, and see what comes next." she explains. "If you constantly concentrate on a five-year plan, then you might miss an opportunity to do something far more interesting. Everything I've done that's been exciting was never planned."

In recent years, Rice has devoted much of her free time to projects such as the Center for a New Generation. "It's a nonprofit after-school program to provide educational enrichment for kids in East Palo Alto, California," she shares. "Some friends and I founded it in 1993. The idea is that if you give kids in underprivileged circumstances hands-on support in math, science, language arts, and music, then they'll have every reason to achieve. I was given that as a child, and I try very hard to pass that on."

Like her parents, Rice is convinced education is the key to success. She speaks at college campuses around the country, telling students, "In America, with education and hard work, it really does not matter where you came from; it matters only where you are going."

Rice defines freedom as "the opportunity to soar as high as you possibly can. It means people are not going to judge you or put a block in your way because of how you look, what language you speak, or where you came from. But freedom is not the ability to do anything you want—that's a misrepresentation. There is a responsibility that comes with freedom: to use it well."

A ROLE MODEL

Over the years, Rice has received many awards and honors for her extraordinary achievements. In 2002, the National Association for the Advancement of Colored People (NAACP) selected Rice as a recipient for its President's Award, which was presented at the Image Awards ceremony. The Image Awards are usually given to entertainers—musicians, comedians, and movie stars. Rice was recognized as a person who had "advanced the cause of minorities through leadership or example." NAACP President Kweisi Mfume presented Rice with the prestigious

Rice accepts the President's Award at the NAACP Image Awards in Los Angeles in 2002.

award. He noted that she was the first woman ever appointed as national security advisor, and that she had routinely overcome all sorts of bias against women and blacks in her career as a foreign policy expert.

In accepting the award, Rice paid tribute to her parents, who had lovingly supported and encouraged her as a child. "Though Birmingham had its limits, they told me that Birmingham's limits should not be mine," she said. "As I travel with President Bush and as we meet with leaders from around the world, I see America through other people's eyes. I see a country that still struggles with the true meaning of multi-ethnic democracy, that still struggles with how to accommodate, and indeed, how to celebrate diversity. But it's a country that is admired because it *does* struggle to become better. It's not perfect, but it is a long, long way from where we were."

John and Angelena Rice had great expectations for their little girl, and she fulfilled every one. They believed she could be anything she wanted to be, and she has proven it over and over again. The Rices knew their daughter was meant to make a difference in her world. And that is exactly what Condoleezza Rice has done. She has inspired countless others to do the same.

Condoleezza Rice has excelled in her chosen field, serving as an example of how dedication and hard work can bring success.

Timeline

1954 Condoleezza Rice is born on November 14 in Birmingham, Alabama.

1955 Rosa Parks refuses to give up her seat on a bus to a white man in Montgomery, Alabama.

1962 The United States and the Soviet Union come close to war in the Cuban Missile Crisis.

1963 The Sixteenth Street Baptist Church in Birmingham, Alabama, is bombed, killing four young African American girls.

1964 President Lyndon Baines Johnson signs the Civil Rights Act of 1964.

1967 Rice moves with her family to Denver, Colorado.

1968 Civil rights leader Martin Luther King Jr. is assassinated on April 4.

1969 Rice graduates from high school at age fifteen and enrolls in the University of Denver.

1974 Rice earns her bachelor's degree in political science from the University of Denver.

Impeachment hearings against President Richard Nixon begin in May. He later resigns.

1975 Rice receives her master's degree from the University of Notre Dame.

1979 Americans are taken hostage inside the American Embassy in Tehran, Iran, by followers of the Ayatollah Khomeini.

1981 Sandra Day O'Connor is the first woman to be appointed to the U.S. Supreme Court.

Rice earns a doctoral degree from the University of Denver and becomes an assistant professor of political science at Stanford University.

1984 Rice publishes her first book, *Uncertain Allegiance: The Soviet Union and the Czechoslovak Army.*

1986 Rice moves to Washington, D.C., to work on nuclear strategic planning as part of a Council on Foreign Relations fellowship. Rice's second book, *The Gorbachev Era*, is published.

1989 Rice becomes director of Soviet and Eastern Europe affairs for the National Security Council and special assistant to the president for national security affairs during the administration of President George Bush.

1991 The Soviet Union collapses and dissolves into fifteen separate countries.

1993 A bomb explodes in a parking area under the World Trade Center in New York City.

Rice returns to Stanford University to become the first woman, first African American, and youngest provost in the university's 102-year history; serves as its chief academic and budget officer.

1995 Rice's book, *Germany Unified and Europe Transformed: A Study in Statecraft*, is published.

1999 Rice serves as foreign policy advisor for George W. Bush's presidential campaign.

2000 Rice is appointed by President George W. Bush to be the nation's first female national security advisor.

2001 Terrorists attack the World Trade Center and the Pentagon on September 11.

Rice takes a leading role in the United States's War on Terror.

2002 Rice is awarded the President's Award from the NAACP for advancing the cause of minorities through leadership or example.

To Find Out More

BOOKS

Gormley, Beatrice. *President George W. Bush: Our Forty-Third President.* New York: Aladdin Paperbacks, 2001.

McKissack, Patricia and Frederick L. McKissack. *Martin Luther King Jr.: Man of Peace.* Berkeley Heights, NJ: Enslow Publishers, Inc., 2001.

Meltzer, Milton. *There Comes a Time: The Struggle For Civil Rights.* New York: Random House Books For Young Readers, 2001.

Rediger, Pat. *Great African Americans in Civil Rights.* New York: Crabtree Publishing Co., 1996.

Ross, Stewart. *The Cuban Missile Crisis: To the Brink of World War III.* Chicago: Heinemann Library, 2001.

ORGANIZATIONS AND ONLINE SITES

Distinguished Women of Past and Present
http://www.distinguishedwomen.com/index.html

This lively site includes short biographies of famous women throughout history.

The History Place
http://www.historyplace.com

This educational site provides articles, exhibits, and photographs in a "fact-based, common sense approach to the history of humanity" for young Americans and students around the world.

The White House For Kids
http://www.whitehousekids.gov

This is the official site of the White House. It includes photographs and biographies of the President and the First Lady, as well as games, quizzes, and White House trivia.

A Note on Sources

Condoleezza Rice is the one of the first books written about the national security advisor. When I started researching this book, I could not find any other biographies of Dr. Rice. The information found in this book comes primarily from magazine and newspaper articles, many of them written during George W. Bush's successful presidential campaign in 2000. When President Bush appointed Dr. Rice as the nation's first female national security advisor, people wanted to know more about this brilliant and accomplished woman. In-depth profiles appeared in *The Washington Post*, *The New York Times*, and *The National Review*. Dr. Rice shared many personal stories and anecdotes in interviews with television talk-show host Oprah Winfrey and reporters from *Essence* magazine.

Dr. Rice's position puts her in front of the news media daily; she gives press conferences and television interviews on a regular basis. In addition, she often gives speeches at special events. Much of the material in this book comes from written transcripts of her comments.

—*Christin Ditchfield*

Index

About the Author

Christin Ditchfield is an author, conference speaker, and host of the nationally syndicated radio program *Take It To Heart!* She has interviewed celebrity athletes such as gymnast Mary Lou Retton, NASCAR's Jeff Gordon, tennis pro Michael Chang, the NBA's David Robinson, and soccer great Michelle Akers. Her articles have been featured in magazines all over the world.

A former elementary school teacher, Christin has written more than twenty books for children on a wide range of topics, including sports, science, and history. Ms. Ditchfield makes her home in Sarasota, Florida